I0052514

Bruce King and I

Sofia Edlund

Table of Contents

Foreword

Today I run a successful business on the Internet, but the road was long and I stumbled for the most part; mostly, due to poor advice and lack of experience. I wrote this book specifically for those who are starting their own business or already have their own business. To those who want to sell or are already selling their service and/or products and want to build a successful business, this book will share with you my own experiences, because I do not want anyone else to have to make the same mistakes I did.

I bought an audio book written by a sales guru, Bruce King. In his book, he promised that by following his advice, readers would be millionaires within three months. I thought it sounded fantastic and wanted to learn everything about sales. There was a part in his audio tape where he promised his audience that everything in the book worked. Sadly, truth and reality are worlds apart.

It is not enough to want to sell and become an instant millionaire. It is not enough to buy a bestselling book and be a skilled sales person to succeed. Unfortunately, I believed otherwise because I wanted to do everything right by the book.

There are other factors that influence your chances of success. Some of these factors are so crucial that you need to consider them closely before you even get started with your marketing efforts; and more specifically your investment, which in some cases can have devastating consequences for you and your family's finances. The second aspect that easily comes to mind is that of supply and demand, price, trends, marketing, and of course what product you have to sell. King was not very clear on these factors but I plunged on anyway.

For many people, starting a business means a major shift both in work and private life. It takes great effort and incredible courage to move from a fixed income to an uncertain and unstable income. This is even more crucial when you have monthly expenses and bills to offset. You are putting a lot at stake; your family's welfare, financial and social security, and peace of mind.

I have no doubt that books like the ones sold by Bruce King and other gurus such as Max Söderpalm may have worked for others but it didn't work for me. Maybe I didn't know much about marketing and what it takes to sell as they do. I will not tell you not to believe the gurus; I would rather you do due diligence before starting any venture. Whatever you read here is my opinion. There is no way you are going to be a millionaire in 3 to 8 weeks or even one year after reading a book such as the one I did. They just sound too good to be true because it almost always is.

I read Bruce King's book for several months, over and over again. His book was my Bible and I lived with it the first year of my business. I was not rich; I was not even close. What happened was that I got into debt and it grew on a daily basis. I had to borrow money from the bank to start my company and later from my own family. Without them I would have gone bankrupt a long time ago.

What went wrong? Why was my situation bad? How did I survive and surge ahead despite all odds? What did I do wrong and what did I miss? There are countless questions that are begging for answers. Luckily enough I learnt from my mistakes and I'm now able to provide all the answers to my questions. I learnt through trial and error.

I will show you what I did and how you can save hundreds of thousands of dollars and sleep better at night. The book is divided into two parts; my story, my company and how it started. The second part is all about marketing.

"I would like to thank the company Nightingale Conant. Through them I came in contact with writer Joe Vitale, whose books have been and are still today my guide, coach and best friend" Thank you!

My Story

In concluding his audiobook, Bruce King said *"If you follow everything I have shown you in this program and are committed, determined and persistent in applying these techniques; then you simply cannot fail to double your sales fast and become world class."*

It felt so right and I was convinced it was the right path for me. Here, I had a world champion in sales that promised riches if I just follow his advice. I had a product that I believed in and knew a lot about because it has been a part of me for over 10 years.

If you've had a business you worked hard on, you will know what I mean. So, this idea is not something new; it is something I can relate with. I looked at my competitors who were making the big bucks selling the same products I do and I knew I could do just as well. What I needed was just to go out there and sell.

I was excited and happy, full of energy and motivation; I was convinced of my plans. I already saw myself as a successful businesswoman. No one and nothing could upset my plans. It felt right; it was just what I wanted to do in my life; something that I love. Nothing feels better than a company I built with my own hands from scratch. I have a product I was passionate about and that was all that mattered.

Expectation and Despair

"What am I doing wrong?" I thought. "What am I missing in Bruce King's book?" I should have doubled my sales by now. I should have already begun to taste my success.

Time passed and the economy became strenuous. The cost of paying staff wages, taxes, rent and other related costs kept me awake most nights. I began to get really worried and as a result slept poorly; no relaxation tape or technique in the world could help my situation.

I took matters into my own hands and went searching on Bruce King's website for advice or even consultations. I was lucky to get a hold of a website with Bruce King's phone numbers. At last, I was going to get answers to my problems and find out what I have been doing wrong. I called the secretary who with a friendly voice booked me on Bruce King's calendar for a consultation.

Full of expectations, I drove my car to a quiet beach on a Tuesday morning in anticipation of a phone conversation with Bruce King. I wanted a location where I wouldn't be disturbed at all. The sun shone over the quiet waters and without winds to stir things up a bit, the location was perfect for my needs. It was as if I had a date with Jesus.

As expected, Bruce King called and to his credit was quite friendly. He asked how he could be of help to me. Quickly, I told him my story as best as I could. I told him about applying the principles in his book for 6 months with no noticeable difference. What was it that I may have missed?

After the phone conversation, I came off highly disappointed. He did not provide any specific advice to follow. Whatever advice he offered was sketchy at best. He told me to hire a star seller and get involved in home parties to sell my products! He said a friend of his had become a millionaire this way. At a point he categorically told me that maybe the problem was not from his methods but rather from me. Clearly, by his standards I was doing something wrong. I came off the phone with nothing concrete. There and then I realized that I may have to take matters into my own hands and do things a little differently. His methods for some reason did not cut it for me.

What he said was totally different from what I heard in his audiobook. The conversation made me even more confused. I no longer want to be rich. I just want it to pass me by. The conversation with Bruce king gave me nothing concrete to work with; I knew then his book was not made for someone like me. Maybe I am better off looking for something else that will lift me from my desperate situation.

One of the first things I did was sell my products over the internet and not just in Sweden. This appeared to be my salvation and the best solution to my problem. Today, I sell to both resellers and individuals. What I learnt was to follow my guts and not to be too hasty in making decision.

Before you start anything

The best advice for any start-up business is to be prepared. The problem is that most people start off their business without proper planning and cost estimation. Of course you cannot plan everything ahead of time. However, a little advance planning and being cautious is a must. This is especially necessary if your family is going to suffer if things go wrong. It is okay to take risks but it is up to you to set limits to the amount of risk you are willing to take and what you can afford to lose.

Here's my advice:

• Do your research.

Is there a market for your Product and/or Service? Are there companies and businesses that are interested in your services enough to hire you? Make inquiries from people in your niche and know the business outlooks. Do you have an edge over your competitors? Do you have a product that is in high demand and is not already flooded? Can you create your own market? Are there things others in the industry have not thought of? Find out what customers think. Get references.

• What is the financial consideration?

Make a budget. How much do you expect to spend on your new business? You need to take all expenses into consideration; private economy, taxes, payroll ~~taxes~~, insurance, telephone, Internet, website and so on.

• How long do you expect it to take before you break even? Double that time. It always takes twice as long as you think.

• Test your product and/or service on a small scale first before you go all-in. This way you see if it will work.

• Get a mentor. It is always good to have someone to share your burdens and challenges with. Whoever you choose as your mentor must have been successful in his/her chosen business for a long time.

• Do you need capital? Find out if you need to borrow money, either from the bank or an investor. It is preferable not to borrow from friends as you don't want your friendship to be sacrificed if shit hits the roof.

• Always keep in mind that "if it sounds too good to be true then it usually is". Trust your gut instinct and always ask yourself if there are disadvantages to your new venture. Then compare them with the benefits before you invest money in someone or something.

• Network.

This is one of my best advices to you. You will gain so much information that you would otherwise have to pay for. This way you save money and time. Find groups and people that operate in the same industry or related industries and join them. Exchange knowledge and ideas with them.

• Never start a business with a friend or relative. Nine times out of ten there will be conflict.

Starting Out on My Own

For many people, starting their own business means a major shift in both working and private life. Many people actually believe it is hard when it is not. My mistake was that I didn't seek second opinions elsewhere first. I was probably a bit brainwashed and despite the piled up mistakes and money lost from the company, I decided that maybe Bruce King's had the best plan for me.

I took a loan, rented an office, hired vendors, purchased computers, and even did telephone subscriptions etc. I did everything by the books and went from nothing to a fully functioning company with several employees. I started with an account that was in the reds and never knew I was on a fool's errand; all because I believed so much in a guru that I was willing to take the risk. I guess that was my first mistake.

There are plenty of things I should have done first; like working from home for a start, doing more market research, retaining my day time job and working on my business as a hobby in my spare time. Had I a book like the one you are reading right now my life would have been different.

Your Networks

Your friends and acquaintances are some of the closest networks you have. Try out your products and/or services with them first before pushing it to the wider market. It is important to be careful when doing business with friends and relatives though. It is easy to run into conflicts related to money with them more often than not.

Business

It is your responsibility to find out which business or venture suits you best. This is most important when starting out. There are limited liability companies, partnerships, sole proprietorships and of course, for those that are too lazy to handle all the paper technicalities, there is an option for them as well.

If you think it is too early to have employees, what you are looking at is sole proprietorship. The difference between a sole proprietorship and a corporation is that whereas in a sole proprietorship you carry all liabilities, but in a limited liability company the legal responsibility lies on the company. If your business is going to involve some risks, you are more likely to lean towards a limited liability company. To learn more, please visit the link below:

bolagsverket.se/mg/prospective/start

Public Company

This requires capital investment but protects you from becoming legally liable.

Sole Trader
If you prefer working alone and do not have lot of capital, this is one is for you.

Partnerships
If you are a little short on cash but have others who are interested in joining you in the business, you can pull your funds together and start off a partnership.

Freelance Solution - Testing on entrepreneurship
I recommend you start small when starting your own business. There are companies that handle all billing, payment of wages, security fees and so on. You do not need an F-tax but will rather be working under another company's name. This way you hire your services to those who may be interested in them without undergoing the stress of setting up a physical business with all the trappings that come with it. The way it works is that you sell your products and/or service through this parent company by registering with them. You will only need to pay a monthly fee. This may be the best option for those who want to try their hands at entrepreneurship before starting their own business. It costs about 8% of your invoices to exploit this option. 8% may not sound like much at first but it can become quite substantial once your business starts picking up and you are doing much billing. You may choose to ignore this little setback and just enjoy your work and bill your clients. Examples of freelance companies in this category are Bolagskraft.se, freelance financial and coolcompany.se

Homepage

Once you have registered your company, it is good to have a website so people can find you. You do not need to be a programmer to create a website. Most web hosting companies have ready-made templates and all you need is to fill in some text and add your images. Your domain is important and should be relevant to your business or company name. Build several cheap websites with good domain names and then decide which one makes the most money. Selling products on your website will present no problems to you at all. There are several payment processors you can use to process your orders and payments right from within your website. You get your orders from your website and emails and then you process those orders and dispatch your goods and services. If your product is unique, there is nothing stopping you from selling it all over the world. To make the process easier, it is better to have your website translated into popular languages of the world.

When you don't have your own idea

Find a product

If you don't have your own finished product, find one to sell. Everyone wants to make money but not all have a finished product to sell. There are several ways to find products. For example you can go into http://alibaba.com; this website details all factories and dealers of several products in China. These factories are where the products are being manufactured. Follow your gut feeling when choosing a product; be sure to compare different factories and ask for quotes. Be sure you are dealing with the factory directly and not an agent or 3rd party. Agents and 3rd parties make the product ~~to be~~ more expensive. Some factories will refer you to an agent. If this happens, you need to decide whether to continue with this company and its agents or find another one.

When you find a product you are comfortable with, don't rush into making all your orders right away. Start by ordering samples and see if this product is what you expected. Usually, the factory you are buying from will want you to pay in advance and also pay some shipping fee. The type of shipping you choose depends on how fast you want the product and how much you are willing to pay for it. The company will usually explain this to you.

A good way to decide on a product to sell is by following trends as they occur in Japan and the U.S. What is trending in both countries will not reach Sweden right away. And so you have some time to order the products and make a huge sale when it gets to Sweden. You can easily monitor trends by subscribing to magazines, children's programs and news channels. This usually gives you a head start.

You can learn from the success stories of others. A good case in point is the story of a German embassy worker's wife whose husband is always away. The husband is the family's breadwinner; they are well off but she was bored. One day, she received an acupuncture mat which sold very well in Sweden. She got curious and contacted the company to become an agent in Germany. The rest was history as the business became a success and she eventually earned more than her husband. These are the stories you should look for in foreign newspapers. Success breeds success and can be copied.

When you find a product

Follow the trends or create them yourself. There are products that you can sell over the internet through your website, auction pages, and social media and so on. You can create hype around your products so that they become trending items over the internet. You may decide to give away gift items to those who buy your products. This is a good way of advertising your products and rewarding your buyers.

Create an App

There are lots of ways of making money by building your own apps. A visit to Google Play store will give you a good idea of the many apps there are on the market today. While it is true that game Apps sells most, but other types of apps can also bring you the big bucks. There are a variety of Apps out there like those that can help you lose weight, motivate, train, life coaching and a host of others. It lies on you to think, add a little bit of ingenuity and think of something that people want.

Sometimes, building an App can be quite expensive but with proper planning you can get around this hurdle. You may decide to learn how to program and build the App on your own. If you have money you may also hire a programmer to build you an App. If money is going to be an issue, you many decide to look for someone who is willing to invest in your Apps. There's no point going greedy. With a good App and investor, you can make a massive sum on 100, 000 downloads of your App even if your share of the profits is just 20%. Who knows, your profits may even run into millions if you do your homework well.

Setting

It's not enough to be a star seller to successfully sell your products.
According to the audiobook I listened to, you can sell your products over the phone but it does not exactly tell you how. Granted that you may be given step by step plans on how to think and act to become a great seller but that does not mean you will be an instant millionaire. To be honest, how many of us are even great sales persons? Like everything else in the world, it requires hard work for you to succeed.

Target

I have a target I wanted to meet; which was to double my sales within a specified period of time. What I did was to put stickers with my targets written on them in conspicuous places in my car, in my closet, on my desk, on the refrigerator door and even in my bag. I wrote down all details of my goals. For example, I wrote down the exact color my new luxury car is going to be and how it would feel to cruise around town in it. I also wrote something about the type of house I would like to buy and so on. My purpose for doing this is to motivate myself to achieve more because if I can see my goals on a daily basis ~~and for this reason~~ I would be more focused on them.

The problem with my well laid out plans is that I focused too much of my energy on the things I wanted without concentrating on how to get them. I should have focused more on my business and divert that energy towards building my business. I was focusing on things that didn't yet exist with no concrete plans on how to achieve them. It is good to dream about these things but it is better to have goals that center around my business; and what steps should be taken to improve on my products, develop the company, and market to my customers. Do this and with time everything else will eventually fall into place.

It is good to have interim targets but dreaming of wealth and money without planning for it is an illusion. The most important thing I learned from this was that everything takes at least three times longer than you planned and that patience really is a virtue. Do not fool yourself. There is no short cut to success; all you need do is work hard.

Affirmation

I repeat my affirmations at least 25 times a day. Today, I still repeat my affirmations even while asleep such that it has become second nature to me. I have often reminded myself that I need to experience my thoughts and affirmations inside of me so that they become real to me.

Positive thinking means you will see solutions to problems instead of seeing just obstacles. In the book that became my bible, there was no concrete advice, no problem solving solutions and real world scenarios to work with. This is where I made my second mistake. I have not empowered myself with skills. In all that you do, you need to devote time for it to succeed. It is always a constant struggle. To avoid being left in the lurch, you need to have a plan B and C.

Do not be surprised to find friends and family come up with negative comments just to discourage you. They will tell you how hard it is to succeed and not to bother setting up your own business. Whatever you do, don't listen to them. Instead listen to those who have achieved success.

Visualization

I set my alarm clock at 5.30 am every day. This is the time I utilize in visualizations while still in bed. I have an audiobook that I listen to and it comes with a music that helps me relax. This audio set is loaded on my mobile and I listen to it every day. It relieves my body and soul from stress. It helps me be more focused on my business and gives me the energy to face each new day.

Visualization is a proven method of controlling our thoughts and I cannot say enough about it. The only thing is that it takes some time before you start seeing results from your efforts. I usually visualize about what my day will look like and what I hope to accomplish before the end of the day. I think of how I'm going to sell my products, about my meetings, campaigns and generally things that will help my business along.

Activity

I avoided every single person that was a negative influence in my life. I tried to be positive by talking to people about how we can change our lives by changing our views on life. I made sure that I'm really happy in all I do. I always avoid anything that would make me sad and empty. I made up my mind not to come up with excuses and blame others. It was a great exercise that really led me forward, and I am grateful for it.

A good idea is to deal with all the things you experience that hardest in the morning, whether it's a customer who complained; an invoice that is late, etc. it's about dealing with your problems and not postponing them. They only become greater the longer they remain and become sour grapes.

Time Management

Time management is one of the topics that are well talked about. Whole volumes have been written about it. Time management is all about managing your time well and choosing to do the right things at the right time. It is about putting the right foot forward and doing things that will benefit you and your family in the long run. Your plans should include things that will help you attain your goals. Disorderliness will only disrupt your plans, your goals and your focus.

SALES

Working on my sales

I started by hiring three sales people, one of whom was new to the business. I followed all the laid out principles in the book. I let my workers go home half an hour earlier. I also gave them copies of the Bruce King audiobook to listen to on their way to and from work. This was part of the requirement during the recruitment process. I bought three cell phones onto which I downloaded the audio books which I gave to each of my workers; making it known that this book will be their bible henceforth. They just could not afford not to follow the steps outlined in the book.

Each Monday, Tuesday and Thursday morning right before work at 8.30am, we would hold a meeting where we would take turns reading from the book. We would discuss portions of the book and how it would make my business move forward. Deep down I know we would face obstacles before we achieve our aims but I had the patience to see it through.

In the beginning, I gave my workers a time frame every week in which they would call customers who they deem to be potential buyers. It was not hard to find these potential buyers as they are mostly customers who retail products similar to mine. Later on I would call them myself to save my staff time and for them to concentrate on the business of making sales and learning the ropes by listening to the master himself; Bruce King.

It was as simple as listening to Bruce King audiobook daily and applying his rules for success. It was easy for us to do while it lasted but therein was one of my biggest mistakes.

Soon I started getting complaints from my sales people about how tedious and monotonous it was going through the book every day. It became a stressful period for me as I had to educate my staff and say the same things over and over again each week.

What I should have done was to start with the sales process on my own first. I would have called and make appointments with the hairdressers and then try and sell my products to the customers myself. I would have tried to monitor things like the prices, quality of the products and hear first-hand views from the customers themselves who are using my products. I should have learnt about my target market first before bringing in any sales staff. All these I would have done and saved valuable time and money.

I even missed an important detail that was not included in the book; consumers. It is easier today for the consumers to buy directly from the suppliers to cut costs and save money.

The sales process
The first week's results were disastrous. We acquired no new customers. Many of our clients asked us to call back at another convenient time. The most popular phrase was "Check back next week".

During the second week I was optimistic something good was going to happen, after all I have been told to call back that week. It was going to take a bit of time to see progress and I was prepared to wait. Patience they say is virtue and it was okay by me to exercise a little patience. This made me stronger and more determined than ever to wait. I meet with my team to record feedback from clients. There was various objections to my products which we noted down in our meetings and we formulated answers which we feel will satisfy our customers and convince them to buy from us.

In the third week, we have customers who wanted to get samples from us. We were only too glad to send them these samples. We included with the samples well written information about us and the products. Because it takes a lot of time to see results from using our products, it was a while before we got feedback from our customers. In retrospect, I realized I would have given out samples to end users and allow them to test it out for us. This way they would become our brand ambassadors. Our niche was a tough one. It was difficult breaking into the hairdressing niche where the market is already flooded with many established products.

The work was slow but we were gradually getting requests for more samples. I felt that the tide was gradually turning and all I needed was patience and forbearance. It was only a matter of time before we began to get new orders. I can visualize it and see it happen soon. I record my thoughts in my book and feel that I'm on my way to success.

Week four passed very much the same way as week three. I had people who only wanted samples, others are only seeking new information and some only want theirs in a distant time. It was a gruelling period for me as I know I had to pay staff salary, rent and other company expenses. With no orders coming in, I have no money to do this.

Month two caught us doing better at handling our daily routines. We felt there was no need for our usual morning meetings and as a result we scheduled meetings at the beginning of each week. What we did was observe trends that we have already read from the book.

By week six, we received our first order. This client was already established in the market and we had to wait some time for their repeat orders. When I talk to other business owners like me, what I discovered was they all have to cope with wholesalers who they compete against; in my own case, it was the hairdressers. Looking back now, I knew I never would have been hasty in my decision to hire staff, rent an office and invested so much in the business. I never mentioned to anyone about the book being my bible.

In month eight to ten, there were a few more minor sales where the customer wanted to test our products. The hardest part during these three months is that when I do some CRM, sales force automation program and saw how my business is doing, the result was catastrophic. Money flowed out of the company and I never did anything to stop it. Had I known my loss would be so great I would have put a stop to it right away.

Bruce King rules and my conclusions

Motivations

I have since learnt that people buy for emotional reasons. The strongest motivation to buy is usually pain and pleasure. The trick is exposing customers to problems or opportunities they never knew they had and showing them how your idea, product or services can help them solve their problems and exploit opportunities and getting them to buy from you. When you call a potential client without first booking an appointment with them, it is called a cold call. Most often a cold call gets rejected for a variety of reasons. It may be that they feel you are rude to them, you are not listening to them, you are cutting off their responses, you are not professional enough or simply because they feel you pronounced their names wrongly.

Personally, I have had to say no to a sales person because I was having a bad day. I refused to listen, even though the seller was friendly. I have also turned down an offer because I could not afford the service or supply.

I have accepted meeting sellers because they have been amazingly nice on the phone. Even though I knew I have no use for the product or simply could not afford them, I booked the meeting just to be nice. I know I am wasting my time as well as that of the seller by agreeing to a meeting. Usually I promise to get back to them at a later date after I have discussed the product with someone else.

Your office and the environment also play a role in how you feel and respond at each given time. It can also affect your confidence.

It is good to know about your potential customers before deciding to contact them. Too many times I have received a positive feedback from customers when I start talking about their business, history or background. It pleases them, and makes them more willing to hear more from me.

Documentation is important

Having a statistics on all calls and on-going sales is important. You do not need an advanced system to make this happen. It may be enough to document what you have done on paper. I run a system where I have ready information on daily sales and that of my three sellers. This means I will be knowledgeable about what my sellers are up to and have a general idea of how things are going in the business. I bought an expensive and proper monitoring and evaluation system that made it possible for me to have control over everything that was going on in the business. It helped me to review, and later attempt to make crucial decisions in my business.

Preparing to Contact the customer

It is important to know how to capture the attention of your potential customer. We prepared a template for this purpose and try to fill it with replies to questions which we have often encountered from customers. What we are doing is to try to anticipate the questions the potential customer will ask and have ready answers for them. The first sentence should aim at capturing the interest of the customer. I have used the so called 'fool proof' sales letter with success.

Referrals

References are a good way to sell to a new customer. It breeds confidence in the mind of the customer when he knows there are some guarantees in buying your product. If your products are bought by competitors or colleagues it will make the customer will feel safer. Here are five principles you should follow when it comes recommendations and referrals:

If you offer a discount to your trusted customers, you may decide to use the customer's name in your sales and marketing process.

Don't forget to ask for referrals before and after a meeting with a customer. You also ask for referrals during the meeting. Encourage your clients to refer you to people who may be interested in your products.

Social networking

Networking is another method to expand your customer base. As networking has become a rapidly growing industry that is powerful, it is good to be seen in social networks such as LinkedIn, twitter and Facebook. Join groups, and become known as the "expert voice" without pushing your products to their faces every time. Start groups, and promote them on Facebook. Attend various meetings, trade shows, conventions, etc. that are specifically targeted to your niche. Share experiences and give and receive advice.

Facebook is a great platform to advertise on. Either you advertise your website or get people to 'like' the group you started. The advantage of advertising your website is that users can purchase your merchandise directly. The downside is that you do not have control over who visits it. The advantage of people liking your page is that those who liked your page will receive your updates in their feeds. They can also click the links to your products and buy them right from your page.

You should get yourself a page on Facebook and collect as many likes as you can. It is also an effective way to communicate with your customers. Try to give them replies as quickly as you can and do not be afraid of negative criticism. Do not remove the negative criticisms but rather make your answers as detailed as possible and do not be afraid to apologize. A little humility will not hurt; do something sensible with the criticism you get. Criticism is the best way to develop.

When you advertise on Facebook, you will probably learn about pay per click and how to use it. It is always advisable to start with low bids in your PPC campaigns. You will also see how much you need to pay to get clicks. Add also a cap on how much you spend on advertising every week. This way you control your spending and will not pay more than you can afford.

NLP Technique
NLP ~~technology~~ is a very interesting technique which shows how we can influence each other unconsciously. This technology, I strongly believe

and feel will help us improve and facilitate communication with others by understanding how the other person thinks and makes decisions; and how we can communicate more effectively with them in a way that enables them to understand us better, and we thus can affect their behavior.

The technique is one of many that help us to communicate more easily with others sufficiently. The only thing is that this technique requires a lot of training and exercises.

The ultimate system

Making use of a sales system is a crucial part in the selling process. With a sales support system, I got better handle on the overall statistics, customer acquisition, sales process, prospective clients, how much effort is being made by my sellers to cultivate new and maintain existing customers, budgeting, and much more. Most often, with the sales support system I know the true state of affairs in my business.

This technology helped my business a lot in that I acquired new clients. It also revealed the true state of my business. I thought that in 5 months I would be able to make good revenue. It soon became apparent that all my efforts were barely yielding profits for my business to survive. Sales support system revealed that the relatively large retailers fail to sell my product to the end users, their customers. This is yet another lesson.

Closing a Deal

Ask your client if he/she wants to place an order; if you do not dare ask for an order, you will never make any money. You can control your clients and close a deal the way you want it. The best way to get your clients on your site is by sending them samples. Do not talk so fast ~~so~~ that they have a hard time following you. Do this and you are making it difficult for them to make a choice. Expecting them to answer every single question will soon become tedious to them and will invariably lose you sales. Talk to them quietly and allow them to think over what you said without rushing them. This will make it easier for them to say yes to you.

It is unpleasant to be refused by a potential customer. Of the points mentioned in the audiobook about how to deal with potential clients, I ~~was~~ disagreed with point number 10. This point had it that while you are packing your briefcase, and moving to the door and at the same time thanking your host for their time, you should pause for a moment and ask your host why he has declined your service. At this point your host is very much relaxed and will be happy to answer your question and let you know where you got it all wrong with him.

I see this strategy as being rude and showing no respect for the client and yourself. This implies that you are actually begging the client to buy from you. The best way to really know what a potential client thinks is not by hanging your head and heading towards the door on first rejection, it is by tackling the issue raised by your host and addressing them squarely. If after trying to convince your host to buy from and you have not succeeded, walk up and leave. Do not make a fool of yourself and beg for answers while at the door. The aggressive sales technique mentioned by Bruce King does not cut it for me. If you are not successful with a client, why embarrass yourself at the door? It is either the client buys from you then because he feels sorry for you or he will still say no irrespective of the fact that you feel sorry for yourself.

If you feel you are tough and can weather any storm thrown your way, by all means go for Bruce King's advice; honestly, it may work for you after all. In the end it is about never making the customer feel cheated. If your customer feels cheated, he will never buy from you again. The aim is to have satisfied customers who will repeat their patronage. Satisfied customers will generate you more money than unsatisfied ones. If you have a satisfied customer, there is every chance he will be a repeat customer. It is far easier and effective to sell to existing customers than constantly chasing after new ones.

Two years later, when I listened to Bruce King's audiobook again; I tried to understand what I missed; then I found the answer in the introduction of one of his audiobook CDs where he quoted Zig Ziegler: *"The most important thing is not which system you use. The most important thing is you have a system."* It is the only strategic statement in the audiobook; there was nothing about knowledge of the economy, planning, or even a snippet about customer behaviour and how to approach them about your product. This makes it harder to implement his methods.

It is one thing to sell and receive orders but no one becomes a millionaire after just a few weeks. Even I know that now. There are so many other variables to take into account that are not reflected in most books that promise you the moon.

Selling by Phone

Selling over the phone is an effective method of finding new customers, although it also happens to be very demanding. It is good if you can write a sales template that is an actual representation of yourself, company and products. It is good to be prepared to answer questions about your product; so you should know it like the back of your hand. It usually takes about a week before you have a template that works.

To get good sales results that averages 10 sales per day, you should be prepared to lift the phone 100-150 times a day. It wears you down but the results are rewarding. To keep a tab on how you are doing, it is good to call your customer base after a month and ask how you are doing. Let them know you are willing to offer them a discount if they can provide you with feedback, buy more from you and refer customers your way. This is a good way to generate more sales.

If you do not want to make cold calls yourself, you may consider hiring a telemarketing firm for this purpose. There are several telemarketing companies you can get quotes from. If using a Swedish company is going to be overly expensive for you and drain your pockets, you may consider going for telemarketing companies in Malta. Their services are far cheaper than what is obtainable in Sweden.

Telesales

It is important to analyze your sales calls so can know how you are doing. It will also help you review issues with your business. This is important as you don't want to waste valuable time doing things that doesn't work. You only have a few seconds to capture your customer's interest, so you need to make them count.

Introduction

Your first lines should be very interesting and attractive to avoid potential customers saying, "No" before they even get to hear about your product. You may decide to open with a question. For example, you may ask: "Do you save 3000 dollars per year?" Nobody says no to that and you have a customer who is willing to listen.

Presentation

Having written down your template, it is good to start from it. Say something about customer benefits, other satisfied customers and what they gained from buying your product or service. Ask questions about the client's current needs and situation. Listen and do not interrupt the customer. Respond to customer queries.

Clearing the way

Do not be afraid to market your product and ask if the potential customer would like to order your product. It is advisable to start with a greeting like "Hi" and then ask your questions and then present your product. It is good to keep quiet for a while after introducing your product. Many potential clients will say yes after this either because they cannot handle silence or feel that they are being hard on you by saying no.

Preparation

Write down any questions you usually get and have ready answers to customer objections. This makes you more confident and you will feel more like an expert. If the customer has a question you cannot answer, be honest, tell them you have to find out and came back with the answer as soon as possible.

Setting

Be enthusiastic. A good tip is to sit up straight and force yourself to smile when you call. Your manner and attitude will be felt through your voice. If you are sitting hunchbacked with negative thoughts swirling in your head, it will be easy for the person on the other end of the line to pick this up. The two tips mentioned above will help you increase your sales. Also be careful not to have lots of sounds around you. Have your cell phone on silent and do not play with your pen or something similar. All sounds that may interfere with the conversation become annoying for the customer. Same thing happens if you have favorite words or expressions. Avoid saying things like "uh", "huh", "ehhh", snorting, coughing, chewing gum or anything else that will be easily picked up on the phone.

Notes

Write down whatever the customer says during the call. This will help you not to forget it later on. Things you write down can be as simple as his going to Egypt for a week and want you to come back after that or other personal details or questions about your product and/or service. When your potential customer hears you mention about your repeat visit, he will feel more special because you remembered all he said. It becomes more difficult for the customer to say no then.

Internet marketing

It is not so difficult to make money on the Internet. It's all about marketing and getting your butts off the seat. Most people want to earn more money but due to ignorance and laziness it becomes really hard for them to do so. It may also be they have a website but are having difficulty getting visitors. Does this sound like you?

My best advice is that you have a page in English, and then in multiple languages. Do not concentrate on the Swedish market alone. If you want to make lots of money, you need to think globally.

You will notice that this book is quite short and gives you links where you can read more about methods and strategies you may find useful. I kept it short by a good reason; I want to get you started right away. The more text there is, the longer it takes you to get started.

Follow the steps outlined and learn while you get started. Many people want to read more text forgetting that they waste more of your time. The sooner you get started the sooner you will start making money and the sooner you will build more pages and make even more money!

Here I will show you how to:

• Get paid.

• How to find your dealer.

• How to find advertisers.

• How to promote your site FREE.

• How to find products / services to sell.

• Why it pays to have a page in English, and how to get it translated into several other languages for FREE.

• Where to find FREE software for your business.

• How you can set your page on autopilot and make it work for you even while you sleep.

• How to get a book published.

• How to find an Agent.

• And much more!

Where is the money?

You either earn money from advertising, subscription or sales. You get paid in checks or directly into your bank account or in an internet account. If you have read this book and follow the steps outlined, you will have come a long way. But you need to devote time and effort in the beginning for something to happen. So please, for your own sake, take your time and do the steps right away and do not procrastinate. In just one week, you can have a page that you can earn anywhere from a couple hundred dollars to $50,000 or more per month. Start from step one and get a product; let it be a learning experience. It will cost you 300 to 400 dollars to kick off with a website and you will earn back the money within a month or sooner. YOU HAVE NOTHING TO LOSE!

Project - Writing a guide, fact book or something similar

Writing a guide can take a day or weeks to write, and it can contain anything from one page to thousands of pages. The beauty of it is that EVERYONE can write a guide and it does not require much. People need information and there are lots of things you can write about. For example, you may write on topics like:

• How to sell your house without a broker

• How to write a book

• Buying a house

• Losing weight

- Becoming Debt Free

- Investing

- How to make Money Playing Poker

- How to record a movie

- Photography

- How to start a forum, community, portal, etc.

- Improving self-esteem

- Guides

- Adventure

- How to get out of an abusive relationship

- How to become rich

- How to get a job

- How to become an artist

- Buying car

- Learning an instrument

- Computer game guides

- Programming

• Security

• How to raise children or dogs

• The meaning of life

…and so on

As you can see, the possibilities and topics are endless. You may think you know too little about a topic but do not forget Google. You can always rely on your experiences if you are too lazy to spend countless hours searching information over the internet. We all have experiences and are born with one talent or another. Now it's up to you to sell your talents. I have a friend who sells information on an A4 sheet in PDF format on where to find an offshore bank that is safe and anonymous. He sells this information for $24 on the internet which gives him a nice little extra income of about 500 dollars a month. Think about this and then multiply it by all the other subjects you can comfortably talk about. There is a general consensus that a decent e-book can generate approximately $ 3,000 per month with weak marketing. If you have 2-3 books, you can figure out for yourself what you could earn. If you are thinking of writing fictional books, start by writing the various chapter headings so that the structure and layout is creative. This makes it easy for you to write the actual book faster. Hone your skills by writing repeatedly so you learn to write the right way.

How do you write an eBook?

It is not at all difficult to start writing your first eBook. Most of us have Microsoft Word in our computer systems. It is a good idea to start off with it. Let me show you how this book you are now reading is designed. It was easy for me to insert the page numbers in the "insert column". All you need do is click on that link and find the column that says "page number". Click on it and place the page number where you want. Often it will give you a variety of options to either insert the page numbers on the header or footer.

Text

The text should be in font size 12 or 14. Font face should be Verdana or Times New Roman. You also be able to paragraph your write ups to make it easy to read. It will also make the book you are writing to appear more substantial. You should also put your web addresses in hyperlinks so it will be easy for the reader to look up the addresses. Hyperlink function is found in the middle of the toolbar; it is shown as a globe with a chain link.

Headlines

The size may be 14 or 16 and in bold. This allows the reader to quickly get an overall idea of what a section is about and make the section easier to find.

Copyright

This is an important part of your book and should always be set.

Frame

Click "Format", "Borders and Shading" and then under the "Border," select "Block," and do this throughout the document.

Create PDF files

When you are done, you have to make it into a PDF file. Almost all Word programs have that feature. Even OpenOffice has it. It is located in the archives and under the "save as".

Others

Time

You can combine your other daily activities with writing. All it takes is to create some personal time for yourself. Decide how much time per evening or day to write and stick to it. It takes time to write a novel, a guide on the other hand can take up to a week. For example, I write 5-10 A4 pages per day. It's all about discipline. This book you are reading took 9 days to write.

Language

Write your book in the language that you are most comfortable with. Then find a translator in the language you want to get it published in. There are a cheap alternatives and it can cost around $5,000 to get it translated. A professional translation agency will charge per word and the payment may be upwards of $50,000.

Often, you may have to present your book in exhibitions but you can also get agents and publishers to help with your book.

Project guide

If you do not want to use Clickbank or similar services, you may want to contact newspapers about advertising your book. Or you may also want to sell them your book. It takes a relatively short time to write a guide. Your guide book should be supplemented with photographs and fact boxes. If you decide to sell the rights to your guide, you will get paid a fixed sum after which the book no longer belongs to you.

There are two options open to you. You can decide to sell your work entirely to a buyer for a sum. Then again you can also write a similar book on an entirely different topic and retail it.

Travel the world and get paid for it

Why not write travel articles? I know several people who travel the world with a camera and notebook always ready. They live and eat for free and earn money from their writing. In the beginning they may have to foot the bills themselves before they have articles published. These articles arc used later as resume towards other countries and hotels.

The best part is that many of them write several articles in different angles and each story comes with different images. Then they basically sell the same story to various magazines and websites. Some also have knowledge of several languages and will sell the same story to even more people.

All you need is a laptop, a camera and a little vacation. Then, contact the various newspapers and present yourself as a freelance writer. If you are successful, newspapers and hotels will call you instead of the other way round.

Project Equity Publisher

To start your own publishing house is not difficult but takes some time. You publish books via print on demand. Create a website for the book and yourself. Then market the book and your page. There are sites on the internet whose mission is to help writers sell and publish their books for example: www.books-on-demand.com/index.php and www.vulkan.se.

The same type of services is also available abroad. Cafepress.com, lulu.com and blurb.com are some examples. You may also Google phrases like 'print + your + book'. You will find several other leads.

Be sure to take your book to libraries; they can order more copies and you earn a commission each time someone borrows your book. You may not become an instant millionaire, but your book has been made popular.

You can also touch up your books in-house. You may print 10,000 books costing 10-15 dollars per book. Get quotes ideally from Denmark or Baltic where printing is cheaper. You can then contact bookstores, gas stations etc. They pay you in arrears when your book sells. It is good to support your book with good advertising and reviews.

Project Blog

There are several reasons to blog. You can force yourself to write just a few pages. You will likely get comments on your writes ups which will help you improve. You may be lucky to get publishers who are interested in your writings and pay you to advertise for them on your blog. You will earn a bonus income from advertising and affiliate sales. Be honest with your readers about your reasons for starting the blog. Write a press release about your book. Readers will often follow up on it. Never mind that many are going to reads your book for free; you will make up for it later.

Making money on the Internet

There are several ways to make money and you do not even need to have your own product.

The options open to you are:

Own product / service

Here you have your own e-book, software, portal, product, website or the like.

Other people's Product / Service

Here you are an affiliate (reseller) of someone else's e-book, software, game page, product, portal or info page.

Blog

This is when you have a blog where you write about your life, hobbies or something similar.

Portal / info site

This is more like a collection page for a particular genre such as games, finance, dieting, etc. where you gather several companies' pages and links. They pay you to put their information on your portal and if they choose to advertise with you, you also charge more for your services.

Pricing - How to sell more by raising your price.
Most of us would probably sell at the prevalent market price compared to what is obtainable in the book store. If you are selling a novel or something similar, it is only right that you sell at the prevailing market price.

However, if you are selling an e-book or software then you should probably put on your thinking cap. For example, let's say you sell an eBook on how to make a million in a year. These secrets are revealed only to you and nobody else. These secrets can only be obtained from you and nowhere else. Would you sell it for $27 or $97? What prices do you think will generate the most revenue?

It's quite a simple case of psychology and mathematics. The low price subconsciously tells the buyer that this offer is for everyone and that the book is not as exclusive as promised. On the other hand, the high price shows that it really is about quality and the secrets revealed are quite expensive. If you buy the cheaper book, you will always wonder what is so special about the more expensive book and if you maybe made a mistake with your choice. Until finally, you buy the more expensive book.

Had you buy the more expensive book first, you will hardly have to worry about the cheap the book. You will tell yourself that you did the right thing. It follows that a high end product is assumed to have a higher value. It may not always be true but that is psychology at work and it almost always works. Additionally, you can earn more by selling the more expensive book than when you sell the less expensive one.

If you are going to sell your secret quality information book at a cheaper price, be sure to mention this on your page and say why. Speak clearly about your book and mention that it has the same information as the scandalously expensive ones. You may want to mention that you do not see any reason why your visitors should pay their hard-earned money for the same information.

Never lower your price. A buyer who a week after their purchase sees you lower the price by $10 will feel cheated. So before setting your price ensure that there is room for you to raise your price later on rather than lower it. I once had a book that I was not happy with the number of sales it generated. So instead of pressing the panic button and dumping down the price, I raised it a lot by $40. Suddenly, the book sold 6 times more. Why the heck did I lower the price in the first place?

The right price

For some reason, the price you set depends on the final figure on your price. For reasons which I cannot fathom, the number 7 sells faster than the number 9. For example, a product that is set at $27 sells more than the one set at $29. I have tried to sell books that end with other numbers such as 5 and 3 but it is the number 7 that sells best.

Selling with warranty

No one wants to feel cheated and everyone wants to have a sense of security. Face it, most will not use a warranty if they feel that your book is reasonable. You can even have a three month warranty but not too many will use it. The most important thing is that you will sell more.

Monetizing a free book / software

You need to prioritize! There are many free books on the internet, where the aim is to attract visitors and collect e-mail addresses. Either you can earn money from advertising and/or affiliate links or you earn money from a newsletter, more about this later on in the book. I want you to think about writing a mini-guide or something close to it.

The difference between ads and text links

Most of us are tired of the so-called banners (ads) and this makes text links more relevant. So should you advertise on a blog or website, it is often more advisable to do so with text links than banners. In a blog it is always best to place your link in your blog posts. This will make your intensions to earn an extra buck less suspicious to an unsuspecting eye.

The same applies to websites. To place a text link in an informative post generates more clicks than a flashing banner.

Make money posting on forums

Do you frequently visit various forums without getting paid for it? One thing ~~we~~ should be clear to us. The forums are making money and rely on its members to generate ad revenue. I have friends who on ~~the~~ average make between 2000 and 3000 entries per year. Why not make some passive income while you are it?

You can do this by inserting a text link with a short description in your signature. This way all those who either hate or love your posts at any time will click on that link in an attempt to find out more about you as a person.

What you do is sign up as a reseller / affiliate of any website with this option. The best deals are the ones where you receive on-going commissions on every person who clicked on your link and then purchase a subscription or membership.

A good example is gambling websites where you have a commission on any game someone plays. The downside of gambling websites is that there is huge competition and most are already registered. This means you have to be a bit clever by having a little knowledge about the industry to know which have the attractive options.

So take the time to find the "right" product or service. Of course you can also have several different products but do not make it TOO obvious. The forums have a tendency to look down on the competition.

Rules

NEVER write your link in any of your posts. It will count as spam marketing and you will get banned. Do not PM others users on the forums about your link. You will be perceived as unserious and will perhaps be reported as spammer.

Finding the right product

The most effective is to find a new product or service that is currently hot and attractive. When this products starts to cool, continue with the next available product that is currently hot.

The other option is to find a niche product with one or few people that cater to that niche in the market. The only set back is that you have to find the buyers who are interested in this niche; these you can find on various forums. Below are some affiliate players in Sweden.

Affiliate Program

For e-books and software see Step 1

Swedish websites with affiliate programs:

www.agentinteractive.se   www.zanox.com/se/   www.tradedoubler.com
www.double.net   www.affiliator.se   www.agentinteractive.se
www.affiliatedpartner.com

Creating your own affiliate system

If you have your own product and want affiliates to help you sell it, you may want to get your hands on professional software. The one I can

recommend is the most reliable of the lot.
http://www.marketingtips.com/assoctrac/t.x/998806

Let us start

I know I posted this before but it bears repeating. Nothing happens in a day. If you are planning to see success in a month, it usually takes twice that much to see it materialize. Therefore, be patient but your efforts should start today. Delaying it will only gnaw at you and when you get started, you will find that you have so much more to do and you will wish you had started earlier.

So start now whether you know what you want to do or not. You do not need to have a product before you can become an affiliate. Remember you are still learning the ropes and will be earning a good income on the side.

I have a friend who was in a similar situation. He wanted to start an internet casino but did not really have the money for it. Meanwhile, he started an affiliate site for poker. Three years down the line and he has given up the idea of a casino. It is not because he was not making good money to support his dreams but because he earned so much money being an affiliate. He has about 15 different sites and works for an hour a day but earns over $100,000 per month. So think of it as an investment that steadily generates money.

DAY ONE

If you already have a product and/or service and are just looking to learn marketing then go to Step 5. If you have an idea but no website yet so go to Step 2.

Step 1 - Find a product or service

Visit http://www.clickbank.net to find pages you can promote. Do not analyze too much, but choose one you think is sensible and are relatively highly ranked or a very new niche. Pick a product or service now, and strategize later.

ClickBank

This is a platform for digital products and services such as e-books, newsletters, subscriptions and software. They take care of everything when it comes to credit card payments, refunds, and placing orders. All you need to do is to start a website and market it. They take care of all the logistics and send you payment via check twice a month.

You can track your sales on their website in real time, and given that they have one of the world's largest dealer networks, they are able to get a hold of several dealers without much effort.

It is important to note that can you also create a dealer page where you will be provided with information on how you are doing. You will have access to finished banners and text links that you can quickly apply on your website, blog, email signature or forum signatures.

Signing up as an affiliate on Clickbank

You may decide to start a poker or casino site. You make money around the clock and the only work you do is to advertise your website.

Another good way is to make an info page / portal or blog on a topic that interests you and which you are sure will interest people. Please write a book or guide that you either give away for free in order to collect email addresses and sell. We all have something we are good at or know a lot about. Topics that generate interests are ranked in this order:

1st – Game,

2nd – Sex,

3rd – Money,

4th – Fashion,

5th - Gossip,

6th – Love,

7th – Trips,

8th – Child,

9th – Sports,

10th – Food,

11th – Animals,

12th – Health,

13th – Cars,

14th – Furnishing,

15th – Garden,

16th – Property

You can also earn money through ads, text links, sale or resale. More on that later in the book.

Find a product
Visit http://alibaba.com or surf around sites abroad that sell products that have become trends. Contact them to become their agent in Sweden or Scandinavia.

Step 2 - Create a Domain
It is ~~much~~ preferable to register a .com domain. Unfortunately, it is difficult to get the domain name you want as there are many who are already occupying that name. If you register a domain with your product or service's name, there is every probability that your domain will end up higher in the rankings. The name does need to be short and easy to remember. The key is ~~to~~ for people to understand what your website is about.

WARNING! Do not use a website where you are offered a free domain name. After a year, you will be offered the opportunity to buy off the domain name for over $500. Should you use a different provider than the one I recommend, make sure YOU own the domain and not your provider.

Step 3 - Making a Website

So, now you have a product and a web space with your own domain name. You need to create a website. Take it easy, it's very simple. Most web hosting companies have ready-made templates you can use if you are just starting out. If you want more professional looking website, there are other pre-made templates you can use. Most of it is just click, enter text and insert the pictures you want.

If you need free wallpapers, and pre-designed templates that are ready made, you can check out

www.freewebtemplates.com; they have hundreds of free backgrounds for your use. If you want a custom web template that is tailored and unique, you can buy them from this website as well.

There are also many business solution templates you can use if you want to sell products on your website. It has room for payment options and you usually ~~you~~ do not need to be a programmer to implement them on your site. My recommendation is that you use the services of a professional once you have your feet on the ground and have started earning some income.

Photos

Remember that when you download pictures from the Internet and use them on your page that it doesn't stop there. Most pictures on the internet are right protected and you would need permission before using them. Instead of getting sued for using pictures you have no right to, it is better to use free images. There are sites that offer great free images. Google "free + pictures."

Text

Before going live with a website, it is extremely important that you proofread all text and also get someone else to do it for you. If your page is filled with typos you will be perceived as unserious. This does not apply strictly to blogs as it does to websites but it is important in all webpages all the same.

Another important thing is that you include contact information on your page. It may be your phone number, company address as well as a contact form to get in touch with you. It is easy for your website to be perceived as scam without this information there. If you decide not to have your phone number on your website, it is important that you keep track of all email you receive and reply them accordingly. If you reply late to enquiries you may lose sales.

What should a page look like?

If you decide to sell only eBooks or software, a unilateral website will do. You can have a page for each product you have on your website. It may get a little complicated to keep track of but it will help you sell your products better. You can also promote several pages of your website and make them more search engine friendly.

It is possible to have a multipage for all your products but you can also keep all your products in one page. Rule number one is to keep the site as simple and clean as possible. Visitors hate to hunt for information that should be quick to find.

Unilateral page

It is important that your visitors not click on several links before arriving on the page of interest. It is good to have all the important information about your products and services on the same page.

In step 1 I talked about picking a product to sell. All information there also applies here.

Top of the page

You have about 5 seconds to keep the attention of a visitor to your page. You should keep your Product / service's main points where they can be seen at the top of the page. The best way to look at it is to put yourself in the shoes of your visitors. What do you want to see when you visit a website?

Photos

It may not be a good idea to keep heavy images that will make your website load slowly. Your images should connect with your visitors and be attractive so they don't get bored and move on to the next website. Don't forget to refer your repeat customers to your website and ask them to refer you to others. This will help you get visitors faster to your website.

It is a terrific idea to give your visitors the opportunity to order early. Do not be afraid to ask a visitor to place an order. Be sure you have an "Order Now!" or something similar where they can be seen on your website.

Affiliate Page

If you sell someone else's product, make sure that your web page for it is not too long. Keep it informative and simple but be clear about the fact that you are using affiliate links on your site. Once a visitor clicks on any of the links it will be registered for you on the parent website and you get paid when a visitor makes a purchase using the links on your webpage. Many companies using affiliates have already made articles and sales pages that you can just copy and replace their links with your unique affiliate link.

Keyword

Keywords are what will bring your website to the attention of the search engines. Keywords are words or phrases that search engines associate with your website. There is also a descriptive text that you can use to briefly say what your site is about. This descriptive text should not be more than 200 words. There are those that are of the opinion that search engines do not care about descriptive texts. You don't want to take any risks anyway so just make sure you add it. Major search engines keeps their search criteria close to their chest so we can only say what works for the majority of people.

Examples of meta-text:

<Meta name = "keywords" content = "poker, holdem, hold em, poker robot, poker tips, poker strategy, poker tactics, freeroll, freeroll, allin, all in, all in, turnkey poker, turnkey casino, starting poker site, start casino

site, PokerPro, PokerPro's, poker babes, poker software, 3d poker, 3-D poker, bluffing in poker, bluffing in poker, poker bluff, pot odds, poker chart, poker charts, wsop, poker profit, free poker book, free poker ebook, tony kein, phil ivey, jennifer tilly, tilt poker, rake, rakeback, poker tactic, blackjack strategy, blackjack tactic blackjack chart, elimination blackjack, EBT, ubt, poker tournament, poker tour, betting tactics, betting pro , betting charts, sports betting, free blackjack book, free blackjack ebook, work from home, make money, easy money, bonuswhore, bonus hunter poker State, poker school, count cards ">

<Meta name = "description" content = "free poker book - Become a PokerPro in 7 days ">

It is advisable to search for keywords that are particular to the service or products you offer. Take a look at the pages that are at the top of the search engines. Once on their page, click on the top of the menu "View" and then "Source". Now the page will display their codes and high up on the page, you will find the Meta name and description. Copy and Compare the different highly rated competitors in order to determine your own keywords. Read more in step 5.

Niche keywords

Take a word like 'poker', if you search for the word in Google, you get about 244 million hits. Trying to make it to the top with that keyword will be extremely hard especially if you are new to that niche. The trick is to go for keywords that people search for but which are not so popular that you won't get a chance of making it to the search engine front page if you try. If only a few webpages have the not-so-popular keywords, the better for you. There is a chance of you making it to the top of the search engines if you use such keywords.

There is a website where you can get free information and also do free keyword searches; wordtracker.com. You can briefly search for keywords which people are looking for but which are not being used by too many websites or competitors.

To learn how to test your keywords, visit Wordtracker.com. They also offer a paid service which gives more accurate information.

Another thing that search engines like is the text in the blue bar at the top of your browser. Be sure to put enticing text there. It doesn't necessarily have to be the name of your product, book or page. Put your most important keywords where they can easily be found by the search engines. When a user inputs those keywords in a search engine, what they will see is your websites. You can see that good keywords matters a lot.

Blog

When you buy a domain name and web hosting; you automatically get the option of using several blogging platforms. Search engines like blogs that are constantly updated with new information. You should post at least one article per day to get good rankings at the search engines. I will talk more on blogs later in the book.

Free Is Good

Below are useful free services that can help you with your website:

Manufacture banners

www.bannercreator.nu / banner maker.html www.banner-generator.net/

Free templates

www.frewebtemplates.com   www.oswd.org/   www.zymic.com/free-templates/

Free images and graphics

www.freegraphics.com

Free Image Manipulation Program

www.gimp.org

Step 4 – setting your web page on autopilot

It is estimated that it generally takes up to 7 follow up emails before someone decides to buy from you. If you decide to do everything on your own and continually monitor your webpage day after day, you will waste lots of valuable time and at some point you will simply get fed up. There is a way round this problem; by setting your page on autopilot. It will give you time to relax and take care of yourself.

How it works:

When a customer signs up for your free newsletter, and / or to get a free offer / mini course, you will have the opportunity of collecting their name and email address. This email goes to a third party website which immediately sends an email to the visitor with instructions on how he / she can download whatever information you have to offer. Alternatively, you can decide to be smart and divide the information into 7 parts that is automatically sent to your visitors at certain times of the day or week. You can also block some email addresses like those of your competitors or spammers. If the same email addresses registers twice, the system will recognize this and only send your information once to avoid you being seen as a spammer.

All you need to do is write 7-10 emails and configure how and when the visitor will get them. Once a month, write a newsletter and set it to be sent to your selected email addresses. Some providers have a free and paid version of email responder system. In the free version you only get one account and 5 follow-up emails, and there will also be ads from third-parties. My recommendation is that you go for the paid version. It is inexpensive and you will increase sales by at least 200% - Go to http://www.GetResponse.com/

If you are interested in autopilot programs I recommend you buy one from:

http://www.marketingtips.com/mailloop/t.x/

The difference between the two is that in getresponse your emails are sent from their website and bears their domain name whereas in the second option, any mail you send will bear your website name instead of that of the provider's as is the case in the first option.

Newsletter

Each email you send should end with a tantalizing snippet of what to expect next. This makes it very possible that your readers will be eager for your next email. You can either send your newsletters monthly or weekly. The best days to send them are usually on Tuesdays and Wednesdays. There is a greater chance that your emails will be read on these days.

MARKETING

Step 5 - Search Engines

Most of the traffic to your site will come from search engines; so you need to customize your page for the search engines.

1 - It is uncertain whether the major search engines really utilize the so-called Meta tags on a page, but I still recommend that you put them on. Meta tags are one of many words that visitors usually search for. You can actually have as many words as you want but keep in mind that the words you choose should have something to do with your product / service. Otherwise there is a risk that the search engines will ignore you. Do not repeat the same word several times. You also need to use words that describe the page briefly. I have explained in the previous section how to search for the descriptive text of a website. When you visit a page in your

browser, click on the topic, then "View" and then "source". This will show you the programming text as well as the Meta tags and description.

2 - Review the text on your page. The more the words on your website matches what a visitor is looking for the higher your websites chance of being ranked high by the search engines. You do not want to add irrelevant words and keywords that will not benefit you in any way. Your keywords should match your products and services.

3 - Once you've done this it's time to leave your page to the search engines but before doing that I would like you to make your page appealing by making it easy to be found by search spiders. They go over your pages just as spiders do and read the words on your page. Go to www.megacrawler.com and www.dogpile.com and register your page. It will make it a bit faster for search engines to find your site.

4 - Now you need to register your site with the search engines. Go to the links below and submit your page. The purpose is to help you submit your website to the search engines.

www.google.se

www.yahoo.se

www.msn.se

www.altavista.se

www.infospace.com

www.sesam.se

www.alltheweb.com

www.netscape.se

There are other alternatives that you can find on the search engines. Just Google "search engine + directory." There are also websites that promises to submit your website to all search engines for a fee. It is preferable to manually register your website with the search engines because not many search engines allow automatic registration by robots. In fact some actually frown at it. Some pages are automatically indexed by the major search engines. The higher you are on search pages the higher the probability of ending up high on the charts.

Most search engines offer you a faster registration for a certain fee. If you are in a hurry to be found by the search engines, you may decide to pay for this service. This is applicable to search engines like Google, Yahoo and MSN. If you decide to keep the costs down and are not in a hurry, it may take 4-8 weeks before you appear on search engines for a query.

You can keep track of your rankings and that of others by downloading a toolbar from www.alexa.com. It's not completely accurate but gives a very good idea of how popular a website is. Whenever you visit a page, you'll see how well ranked the page is in your toolbar.

Step 6 - Google Adwords

When you register your domain and web hosting, you also receive a gift certificate for advertising at Google. Click Google Adwords and use the code you received and advertise for your different keywords; the higher the bids, the higher price. Placing low bids is okay as long as you end up on the first page of the search engines. Go to www.wordtracker.com to find the right keywords for your page for free. The more niche words there are, the better the results.

The way it works is that when a visitor searches for your keywords, your ad will come up in the space right below the search bar and above the unpaid links. You only pay if a visitor clicks on your ad. While other search engines have similar systems, it may be worthwhile to purchase advertising space at major search engines like Yahoo and MSN.

Step 7 - Library

There are a variety of sites where you can register your site in different libraries (directory) for free. Search engines also take into account how many other sites link to your page and it is therefore important that your page's link is found on so many other sites as possible.

Register your site in these directories:

www.dmoz.com; www.yahoodirectory.com; www.looksmart.com; www.directory-google.com; www.greenstalk.com; www.somuch.com; www.jayde.com; www.searchsight.com; www.illumirate.com;

www.geniusfind.com;   www.earthstation9.com;   www.linksmatch.com;
www.bigall.com;

You may also search on Google for "directory + free" for more options.

Step 8 - Free advertising - link exchange

There are plenty of sites that advertise your sites for free. Search on Google and type in "free advertising", "free ads", "free advertising".

An example is:

www.classifieldsforfree.com

There are also programs that allow you add other people's addresses on your page. These programs allow for direct link exchange. Here you make contact with websites within your industry and exchange links. Google free "promotion + directory"

Link Advertisement

There are sites that offer to host your links for a fee i.e. link exchange sites. Do not waste your money in such websites. It is like throwing your money down the drain because search engines no longer index pages with links in those sites.

Step 9 - Sell Traffic

There are sites that offer to get traffic to your page for a fee. If you decide to go this route, it is good to start by purchasing smaller numbers so you can measure the quality before you buy larger amounts. It is called "bulk traffic". These are some of the sites to patronize for this purpose:

www.spiralhits.com;

www.easysitehits.com;

www.clickquest.com;

www.trafficdepot.com;

www.guaranteed-hits.com;

www.site-hit.com;

www.4webhits.com;

www.clicks4u.com;

www.trafficswarm.com;

www.trafficg.com;

www.1worldline.com;

Step 10 – Renting email addresses + Safe List

You can also buy email addresses of people who have opted in to receive advertising mails. Here are where to get them:

www.postmasterdirect.com;   www.yesmail.com;   www.focalex.com; http://listdotcom.com; http://yourluckylist.com; http://tripleyourlist.com; http://thelistmachine.com;

You may also register on the so-called safe list. They allow you send email to others who have indicated their interest to receive e-mail with advertisements.

http://www.letsallworkathome.com/pljoin.html

http://www.google.com/search?hl=en&q=safelist+directory

Step 11 - Write articles

There are some sites that offer free articles for webmasters who need materials and articles for their newsletter and website. People write articles and put them on these sites. At the bottom of each article, the author will write his/her signature with his/her name, email address and website. You may also advertise in these e-zines.

www.newsletteraccess.com www.ezinelocator.com

www.emailuniverse.com www.zinester.com

www.gort.ucsd.edu

www.bestezines.com

www.ezinearticles.com

www.freesticky.com

www.GoArticles.com

ArticleDashboard.com

Content Desk SubmitYourArticle.com

www.ideamarketeers.com

www.findsticky.com

You may also try to search for "newsgroups" or "free + e-zine directory" in the search engines.

Step 12 - Press Release

Writing and posting a press release can provide a lot of traffic. Make it short and sweet as if you were a reporter. Examples of press release sites are:

www.gebbieinc.com

www.themegazineboy.com

www.thepaperboy.com

www.pressreleasenetwork.com

www.bacons.com www.mediafinder.com

Another way to reach out in Sweden is to use Newsmill.se. There you can write opinion articles that will appear in your news feed.

Step 13 - Shopping robots

Sign up for free shopping robots. Visitors use them to compare prices. Once you are registered with them, you will get more visitors and buyers. Some are free to register with cheap paid options. It is usually money well spent when visitors click on your site and buy from you. Some also have pay-per-click ads or take commissions in when you receive payment for sales. Shopping robots also increases your chances of being found by the search engines. Below are some examples:

www.kelkoo.se

Free

www.froggle.com

www.pricescan.com

Paid

www.shopzilla.com

www.froggle.com

www.mysimon.com

www.pricegrabber.com

www.shopping.com

Step 14 - Forum / communities

Sign up for the various forums in your niche. Be sure to only offer your tips / opinions that are relevant and helpful. It is important that you NOT drop your links incessantly or write about just YOUR products in your posts. Do not promote your site hard on these forums because it is considered spamming and you will be banned. In your signature, you are free to show your URL and a short descriptive sentence. Believe me, people who like your opinions will click on it.

This method takes a little longer and does not provide immediate sales. It is important to frequently post on important topics so that you will be considered an authority of some sort in your niche. People will also take you seriously and will be more comfortable knowing you are not just there to promote your products and services.

The big advantage here is that your posts will be there forever and appear in search engines. Whenever people search for similar information such as the one you share they will stumble on your posts.

Step 15 - Blog Comments

There are numerous bloggers on the Internet and chances are they have the same views as you and write in your niche too. There are two things you can do to attract more traffic to your page:

Send an email to a fellow blogger and tell him/her briefly about your own blog. Ask if he/she is interested in exchanging links with you. If he has the slightest interest in getting more visitors, your offer will be accepted. It is equally important to remember that you need to have a substantial amount of blog posts and the people you are asking to exchange links with are in the same niche as you.

Alternatively, you can comment on other blogs and state your candid opinions of their posts. When you comment on blogs, be sure to insert your links in the comment. Be careful not to show that you are the one who is directly promoting your links.

Step 16 - Start more blogs

You should consider blogging on free sites like Blogger, WordPress, CNN and others. Add your links to these other blogs. The advantage is that your link appears in multiple places and your ranking with the search engines increases. These free sites will market your blog internally and it will result in more visits. Do not make it be TOO obvious what you are doing.

Google "free + free + blog and blog options."

Step 17 - Start more websites

Build more websites on free services like freeweb.com. It takes you 10 minutes to design it. You will have a private page with your "real" website link. Members' link can be found somewhere on the page. This will help to raise your rankings in the search engines.

Google "free + website + and free website alternatives."

Step 18 - Affiliate System

The absolute best way to get a lot of visits and sales is to start an affiliate system where people can register and sell your product or service. Be generous with the commission; give about 50-70% commission if you have an e-book or something similar. If you are too stingy you will not get any affiliates. A cheaper and easier way is to set up your book on

Clickbank. If you use Clickbank, they have a complete system where affiliates register. Whatever you choose to do, it is important that you not only try to get a lot of retailers, but also help them along by suggesting marketing tips, ready-made banners and text links they can use as well as complete text of e-mail messages or articles they can use. The easier you make it for them the more they get involved.

Bloggers

Get in touch with bloggers who write in the same niche as your book. Your letter should include the following: Offer them the opportunity to be an affiliate for you and write a brief description of your book. Explain how much they will earn on every sale. Explain that it is a secure payment system where they can follow their sales in real time. Explain how to sign up and how the text link is designed.

This way, when the blogger makes a post so they can insert your link in the post so that the reader can click on it for more information. The reader will not see it as an intimidating ad. If you are lucky to get a popular blogger recommend your link, your product will sell faster.

Super affiliates

There are a lot of people who are super affiliates. They sit on a huge email bank and send out emails with your offers and they then earn commissions from each sale. If you get a super affiliate to sell your product or service, you can expect a sharp increase in sales.

Super affiliates know they are really attractive and should therefore be treated with great respect. When you make contact with a super affiliate, it is important that you know/say something about your sales, what commission looks like (it should be around 65-75% to make them interested) and you should also give them a personal free copy.

Remember to NOT explain to them how an affiliate system works; this person is probably more familiar with it than you. Refer him/her instead to your information page.

Step 19 - Make Money

There are several ways to make money on your site that is simple and free; example is when you earn money on clicks and sales.

Google Adsense

This is an advertising program where you paste a code from Google on your site. Each time someone clicks an ad on your site, you earn some money.

IMPORTANT! Do NOT click on ads on your pages or you may be banned instantly.

Affiliate

In your newsletter, website or blog, you can recommend various products or services. You will find products to promote on the links below.

www.cj.com   www.associateprograms.com   www.refer-it.com
www.affiliatesdirectory.com   www.clickbank.com
www.lifetimecommissions.com

Classifieds

The best way to get classified ads on your site is by showing the number of visitors on your site. There are many plugins you can utilize for this purpose. These plugins will also show the number of unique visitors to you website.

Step 20 - Payments

If you have a product / service and you want to start charging for it, it may be outright awkward to starting using credit card payments system right away. It is also very expensive. To bypass this problem, it is better to join a payment processor as this is already a finished system. This will save you some stress. If you have an e-book or software, I recommend www.clickbank.com. They double both as payment processors and affiliate solutions. I will also recommend www.paypal.com for payment processing.

Step 21 - Viral Marketing

This is perhaps one of the most important points in this book. Viral marketing is a term which is easily explained. When people talk about your website and share your links to friends and acquaintances, it is easy for word about your website to spread like wild fire without you spending a dime for it. This usually happens when there is any newsworthy item on your page. Soon word about this news will spread like a virus, hence the name viral marketing.

People will spread news and get their friends to join websites because it pays either financially or is of worth to them in some way. A good example is Skype and MSN messenger whose owners barely need to advertise for members. Today, they have a million industry users and millions of membership.

Other good examples of companies that have made it this way are, Hotmail, ICQ, Facebook, YouTube and others. During their short time they have been visited by millions of people and counting. Visitors can advertise on your site for free or at a very low cost. They can also earn commissions as affiliates. If people are impressed by what you have to offer they will be quick to refer others to your website.

There are ways you can use to make your site go viral. Offer visitors a free eBook or guide on the condition that they give their email addresses. You may even offer them more services for free if they leave three friends' email addresses. Having a "Tell a Friend" form on your page is also useful. Consider Giving out a free newsletter. Offer them a sample of your product free. Make a funny or interesting video clip and place it on your site so that people can voluntarily spread the link and in the process bring visitors to your site. Your web address should constantly appear on the video. Have your affiliates insert your site address in their email signature. Your affiliates can also add a link to your page in their signature on forums. Have a free service where visitors can send a virtual gift to their friends in the form of a postcard, video, etc. In order to get their gift, they must click on your page. Readers can share your blog posts with friends and family. If you have written an article or newsletter, send it to your friends and ask them to share it. You may also send a funny email or an interesting article to friends and customers; ask them to pass it on to their friends. Be sure to make it known that all information on your site is free to send to friends. If you sell your own products, you may add your eBook and other incentives as bonuses to those who buy from you. Contact bloggers, portals, hobby pages etc. and offer to give away your guide through their website or blog. Offer free utility items such as buttons, images, graphics, applications, etc. on your website so that visitors can easily recommend and share with friends.

Submit your guide to websites and libraries for them to be used as free books. Finally, you should know that there are a lot of websites that offer you traffic exchange. Experience has led me to believe that such sites do not offer useful traffic as most visitors are only interested in making money by clicking on your links.

Facebook

On the left column of your Facebook page, you can click to get more information about creating an account for your company or product and get as many people as possible to like it. After you have created your company Facebook page, take advantage of your friends and ask them to like your page.

You may also advertise on Facebook. You do this by paying per click. Facebook will give you a suggestion on cost per click, but ignore it. Often you get suggestions for 11 to 15 cents per click but I have noticed that it is only as good for 3-4 clicks on your page. Facebook can be an effective advertising method if people can receive your posts in their feeds. It is important to post articles and things that are newsworthy as well as those which people will find funny and for this reason like your page. It is also important to make a realistic budget on how much you are willing to spend each week on advertising. This will prevent you going broke.

Off-Line Marketing

You may supplement your internet marketing efforts with offline marketing. Offline marketing can be expensive but they are effective nevertheless. Off-line marketing include:

• Newspaper

• Adverts on cars

• Flyers in mailboxes

• TV and radio ads

• Billboards

• Telemarketing

Start a Personal Blog and make money

It is estimated that a new blog is started every second on the internet. About 40,000 new posts are being made on the internet every hour. Starting a blog means you are facing strong competition. Starting a blog and marketing it professionally is in my opinion the absolute best way to make money if you are lazy but creative. You can work a few hours a week and earn over $50,000 per month. Even if you are in a small niche, you can earn money from your blog. It works best if you can translate your blog into other languages. Here are a few ways to make your blog posts interesting:

- ✓ Be provocative
- ✓ End each post with whatever subject you are bringing up tomorrow
- ✓ Do not be afraid to stand out
- ✓ Update your blog everyday with new posts
- ✓ Be proactive when you receive comments and reply them
- ✓ Invite comments
- ✓ Promote comments that makes sense and adds value to your site
- ✓ Be active on other blogs and forums
- ✓ Write to editors of newspapers and make yourself known
- ✓ Write scoop that other newspapers can quote in their news articles
- ✓ To keep readers interest, make your posts fun, provocative and interesting

Here are top topics that interests people on the internet:

1. Sex

2. Money

3. Gossip

4. Health

5. Love

6. Trips

7. Child

8. Sports

9. Food

10. Animals

11. Technology

12. Cars

13. Furnishing

14. Garden

15. Property

Registering a domain

It is preferable to register a .com rather than other extensions like .edu, .org, .net etc. Furthermore, you may find it difficult getting the domain name of your choice as they may have been already occupied. As I mentioned earlier if you register a domain with your product or service's name, there is every probability that your domain will end up higher in the rankings. The name does not need to be short and easy to remember. The key is to for people to understand what your website is about.

WARNING! Do not use a website where you are offered free domain. After a year, you will be offered the opportunity to buy off the domain name for over $500. Should you use a different provider than the one I recommend, make sure YOU own the domain and not your provider.

You can also start a free blog at Blogger or other free blogging platforms. The snag here is that you do not have the same control as when you purchase a domain and webhosting and again, you can be censored.

Where is the money?

Classifieds

The best way to get classified ads on your site is by showing the number of visitors on your site. There are many plugins you can utilize for this purpose. These plugins will also show the number of unique visitors to your website. The greater the number of visitors to your website the more money you stand to make when they click on your ads. In an advertising system, there is the option of pay per click or pay per number of exposures. Below are some advertising sites you may want to consider.

www.blogads.com

www.chitika.com

Recommendations
Some companies pay well for bloggers to recommend their products or services. They will contact you once you become popular.

Affiliate
Go to Step 1 and sign up for various affiliate programs in your niche. At the end of each post or in the text, add your link.

Get hired
Some newspapers and businesses hire bloggers to work for them. They will do anything to get more visits and also to get their customers to stay longer on their website. They will contact you once you become popular.

Product Placement
When you become a popular blogger, companies pay you to write about their products or services.

What should your web page contain?
Opt-In

One of your most important tools is the opt-in form; used for the purposes of collecting email addresses (opt-in). This makes it possible for you to market to your email list later on. By offering new products and services, you can continue making money off your list. It is best to send them your newsletters for free. You should also offer them some type of bonuses. This is a sample of how to announce your bonuses: "Subscribe to my newsletter to get FREE e-book 'blablabla'".

You should have an offer in at least one conspicuous area on your blog or preferably two. You should supplement with a popup. Most people blocks pop ups on their computers but there is a company that has found a way around it. In fact, pop ups increases sales significantly; so it is a must. Go to http://popupmaster.com. It is a cheap investment.

Sitemap

This is a map of all of your pages; it should occupy a separate page. Search engines like websites to have site map; so it may be advantageous to include them in your website.

Tell a friend

This is a simple method of getting more visitors to your page. Visitors to your site will recommend it to any of their friends and all they have to do is fill in their friend's email address. Their friends will receive an email with the recommendation. In the control panel of your web site, you can create a new email address for your auto responder.

Multiple languages

Unfortunately, we must realize that Sweden is a small country and the market is small. If you want to earn more money, you should also have a page in English. Marketing opportunities becomes infinitely larger once you have alternatives.

If you want to have your site in English or any other language for that matter, you may want to use this FREE website translation service called Babelfish. Go to www.yahoo.se and click on Babelfish to read more. You also have the Google Translate and Bing. They are translation software that automatically translates your page. It can translate texts to languages like Chinese and others. I must warn you that some of this translation software may not accurately translate your texts. If you are looking for more accuracy, have a person who is a native speaker or who is proficient in that language to translate it for you. There are cheap Indian translation companies that offer this service; they do it even for Swedish language. Another alternative is to have a friend or teacher who speaks that language translate it for you for an extra buck.

Blog Marketing

The same marketing rules mentioned in Step 4 to Step 17 apply in this case. However, there are some additions. Subscribe for a blog at:

www.technocati.com

www.blogwise.com

www.blogdex.com

www.blogsearchengine.com

www.search.blogger.com

www.blogsearch.google.com

www.blo.gs

www.boeingboeing.com

www.blogthings.com

www.blog-connection.com/submit-blogs.htm

There are also Swedish sites like bloggportalen.se as well as others.

For more options, Google "blog directory"

RSS

You should give your visitors the option to subscribe to your blog so that every time you write a new post they will receive it in their RSS feeds and emails. You sign up on sites that offer this service. When you register your blog, you get an RSS link that you add to your page. These are websites that offer RSS feed subscription for your websites:

www.publisher.yahoo.com / rssguide

www.newsgator.com

www.rojo.jot.com

www.newsburst.com

www.google.com/reader

www.pluck.com

www.bloglines.com

www.rss.msn.com

www.feedburner.com

Register your blog on different RSS directories like:

www.2rss.com

www.moreover.com

www.syndic8.com

www.newsisfree.com

www.feedster.com

www.rss-specifications.com/rss-submission.htm

Ping

Every time you update your blog by writing a post you will need to "ping" it, which means you are telling search engines that you have posted something new. There is every probability that you end on the list of recent blog posts on your particular niche. The more your blog posts per day the more times you are up there on the charts. Some of the following services forward your pings to search engines.

www.weblogs.com

www.blo.gs

www.technorati.com

www.blogexplosion.com

www.pingomatic.com

www.pingoat.com

www.google.com / analytics

Afterword

In this book, I have put to words my own experience and history; all that I went through when I started and invested in my own business. I'm trying with this book to not only complain but also to talk about what's worked for me and share with you the advice and information that I have gained during my journey as an entrepreneur.

The road was not at all easy. It was riddled with failures and near success syndrome. There were times I felt it was not all worth it. I questioned why I even began in the first place. I wanted to quit and have nothing to do with success. I was this close to giving up all because I had the misfortune of not seeking second opinions after listening to a sales guru. I lost a great deal of valuable time and money. If given the chance to start over again, there are many things I would rather do differently. I would listen to my gut instincts. I would do proper research. I would learn what works first. I would have started small and see where it will all lead me. I wouldn't have thrown in all my resources blindly and loose a lot in the process.

All these are things that would-have-been; things I would have done different. A lot of water has passed under the bridge and I came out of it all stronger, more knowledgeable and wiser than I was before. I am no longer starry eyed believing the world is waiting open mouthed for my product and services. I have gone past that stage to realize that it is not how hard you worked that matters but how smart you work. You have to break the norms sometimes and do things a little differently. At times, you need to behave like a pit bull and bulldoze all obstacles out of your way. Most importantly you need to think out of the box and find what works for you. It is by no means a 'one size fits all' situation. It is important to find out what will work for you.

With all these experiences behind me, I have put together this book to tell you what worked for me. The perspective I approached my business from was what pushed me in the right direction. Do not be taken in by some so called gurus and be robed blind of your hard earned money. Anybody telling you that you can achieve success over night is being economical with the truth. Hopefully, my experiences and advice proffered in this book will go a long way in showing you the way. Don't just take my word for it. Try it for yourself and you will be singing a new tune in no ~~distant~~ time.

I hope that my book will help you save a lot of time and money.

Good Luck!

www.ingramcontent.com/pod-product-compliance
Lightning Source LLC
Chambersburg PA
CBHW041146210326
41519CB00046B/140